A DETAILED STUDY OF MENS REA WITH SPECIAL REFERENCE TO IPC, 1860

VOLUME 1, ISSUE 3 OF BRAIN BOOSTER ARTICLES

ANANYA BRAJESH ANAND

ISBN 979-888521050-8

Contents

Preface

"Start writing, no matter what. The water does not flow until the faucet is turned on".

-Louis L'Amour

Hundreds of students and professors are contributing their work to Brain Booster Articles, we are here to provide ample information about Law and Contemporary issues. Our aim is to provide a platform for today's generation to express their views and ideas on law and contemporary law.

Publication

This research paper is published in Volume 1, Issue 3 of Brain Booster Articles

Author

Ananya Brajesh Anand

CHAPTER ONE

Abstract

The criminal law usually forbids objectionable acts, which is why the evidence of the commission of a crime must be backed up with some evidence of such an act. The commission of such an act can be termed as '*Actus reus*' meaning a guilty act. However, due to the severity of repercussions of criminal convictions, the evidence of intent to carry a guilty act i.e. 'Mens rea'*was* brought into the picture. Both '*Actus reus*' and '*Mens rea*' together form the elements of the crime. However, the current research paper will only deal with the former element of crime i.e. 'Mens rea'. The paper primarily focuses on giving an overview of the doctrineof*Mensrea*anditsseveralcatergoriesalongwiththeiranalysis.Further, the incorporation of *Mens rea* in the IPC, 1860 along with its key components has been discussed in the paper.

CHAPTER TWO

Introduction

Mens rea: Definition

Mens reacomprises the mental elements of the “defendant’s intent”. It is one of the pre-requisite elements as the liable act must be “voluntary” or “purposeful”. *Mens rea* refers to the defendant’s mental state at the time of the commission of an offence, also known as “guilty mind”. It roots from the ancient Latin legal maxim- *"actus reus non-facit reum nisi mens sit rea"* meaning an act cannot be held liable unless and until the mind is at fault. The term ‘*Mens rea*’ allows the justice system under the criminal law to differentiate between someone not intending to commit a crime from someone who intentionally committed a crime and was well aware of its consequences. Given that the criminal law takes into consideration the mental state of a person at the time of committing a crime, however, on the other hand, the rule that a person committing a crime in absence of mental fault will not be held liable still prevails. Another rule is that a person cannot be held liable barely, for having criminal thoughts. It is based on the standard of evidence needed to hold a person liable. The question that arises here is how can a person’s thoughts be ascertained and what sets apart criminal thoughts from idle thoughts? Added to this, the law does not punish criminal thoughts but surely, punishes those who enact such thoughts voluntarily.

Mens reaunder the IPC, 1860

The doctrine of *Mens rea* does not have a vivid application to the offences as mentioned under the Indian Penal Code, 1860, which is codified as compared to the common law which stands uncodified. Nevertheless, the doctrine of *Mens rea* is incorporated in the following two ways-

1. The provisions relating to the state of mind of a person to commit a particular offence has been incorporated in the sections themselves

by making use of words such as "intentionally, knowingly, voluntarily, fraudulently, dishonestly, etc, depending on the intensity of the concerning offence. This means that every offence under the Penal Code somewhat comprises Mensrea.

2. Moreover, the doctrine of *Mens rea* has been encompassed under the provisions dealing with the *'General exceptions'* incorporated under Section IV of the Indian Penal Code, 1860.

Research Methodology

Legal research is mainly bifurcated into types of research methodologies namely Doctrinal and Non-Doctrinal. The current research paper makes use of Doctrinal research methodology to extract useful information for undertaking effective research. Doctrinal research revolves around the question of law on a given topic. It deals with detecting a particular law or legislation concerning the topic and an analysis of the same with a logical explanation in terms of the law. The paper revolves around one of the most renowned doctrines under criminal law i.e. *Mens rea* and its significance under the Indian Penal Code, 1860. It further deals with different categories of mental state and its application under criminal law. Lastly, the general exceptions to the doctrine of *mens rea* constituted under Chapter IV of the Indian Penal Code, 1860, has further been discussed in the paper.

Research Objectives

- To study the *doctrine* of *Mens rea* and its categories along with their analysis.
- To critically analyse the existence of *mens rea* and its significance under the Indian Penal Code, 1860 along with relevant case laws.
- To study the scope of general exceptions for *mens rea* mentioned under Chapter IV of the Indian Penal Code, 1860.

Research Questions

The current research paper aims at finding answers to the following questions -

Q1) Why is *mens rea* a necessary element to constitute a criminal offence?

Q2) What importance does *mens rea* hold and why is it relevant under the Indian Penal Code, 1860?

Q3) When are the several defences against *mens rea* and its implication under the Indian Penal Code, 1860?

Literature Review

The research paper involves data compiled from various sources relating to the given topic - The primary source of information includes data from the Indian Penal Code, 1860 which covers the substantive aspect of criminal laws in India. Sections 96-106 of the IPC elucidate on the General exceptions related to the Right of Private Defence which play an important role in the structuring of the current research paper. Moreover, the Code also provides sufficient information on *Mens rea* and its existence and importance in the IPC. The second most important piece of work referred to was the 'Textbook on Indian Penal Code" written by K.D.Gaur. The author puts forward a comprehensive and in-depth study of the Indian Penal Code with the help of several illustrations and case laws. The author presents a vivid picture of the doctrine of *Mens rea* and its origin. He also explains the maxim associated with it in a quite simple manner. Another source referred to was a paper written by Arshdeep Ghuman titled 'Elements of Crime' that aims at explaining the different ingredients necessary to constitute a crime. The author also explains the importance of *mens rea* during the conviction of a person for committing a criminal offence. Moreover, a detailed analysis of the judicial interpretation of the elements of the crime is also presented by the author in the abovementioned paper. The article titled '*Mens rea:* Mental element in Crime' written by Rajni Negi talks about the origin of *mens rea* and how the principle has evolved over some time. Moreover, the article talks about the incorporation of *Mens rea* in the Indian Penal Code, 1860 and certain terms which mark its existence in the said statute.

Another article titled 'Section 25 IPC–Fraudulently 'written by Muskan Guptaaimsat explains the term 'Fraudulently'. The term is defined under Section 25 of the code and further, the author provides a detailed explanation of the term 'intention to defraud' which plays a key role in the conviction of the accused. The essential elements of fraud have been further explained in the article. The author also provides a brief explanation of the term 'dishonestly' along with explaining the differences and similarities between the two terms.

CHAPTER THREE

Mens rea: A defendant's mental state

Mens reain a general sense refers to a guilty mental state, which either might be constituted with intention or knowledge or otherwise, and the absence of which is a particular scenario negates the intention of a crime. Therefore, no act *per se* is considered to be a criminal act, unless and until the doer of such an act does the act with a guilty mind. The intention does not necessarily include the intention to do any act prohibited by common law or some other statutory law, but it may also belong to one of the two classes. The first being, to do any act which in itself is wrong, standing apart from the positive law, or, it might be an act that is prohibited by statutes and in the common law. However, there is a possibility that the two might co-exist concerning the same deed. In common parlance, "intention" refers to the basis or the inclination behind bringing about a foreseen result and that repercussions are bound to follow due to certain conduct of the person. In the words of Lord Atkin, '*a man is presumed to intend the necessary or the natural and probable consequences of his act; and this presumption will prevail, unless from the consideration of all the evidence, the Court entertains a reasonable doubt whether such intention existed or not.*' For instance, if a man abandons his one-month-old child into some unknown and unsafe place, who ultimately dies, then in such a case, it is apparent that the consequences for doing the act were known to him and therefore, he intended doing such an act. Thus, the man will be held liable. On the other hand, if X, while shooting a tiger, shoots B, who was concealed from A's view, and causes injury to B, then in such a case, A cannot be held liable for causing harm to B. This is because, A did not foresee the bullet hitting B and therefore, it was entirely an act of accident.

To examine *Mens rea,* the following two tests were evolved in the due course of time: *firstly,* whether or not the act in question was a voluntary act of the accused and, *Secondly,* whether the accused had foreseen the consequences and the result of such an act[1]. Nevertheless, a uniform sort of mental state is not ought to be present as an essential for all crimes. *Mens rea* takes into account different colors under different circumstances[2]. A wrongful intent for a particular type of offence may or may not be the same for another type.

[1]Hall Jerome, General principles of Criminal Law, 2nd Edn., (1960), pp. 70-77.

[2]Sayre, *Mens rea,* (1932), Harvard LR, p. 974

CHAPTER FOUR

An overview of Mental State

The state of mind of the defendant in *Mens rea* is divided into three categories. Apart from this, there exists a separate category of crime in, the element of *Mens rea* is not needed known as strict liability crimes. The former is comprised of the following-

1. General Intent–general intent simply requires the defendant to have an intention to commit a wrongful act. It comes into the picture when the wrongful act of a person is reasonably expected to take place arising from the voluntary act of the accused without any sort of specific intent by the wrong-doer. Crimes involving general intent are as follows-

a. Rape
b. Battery
c. False Imprisonment
d. Kidnapping

2. Specific Intent– it refers to a special state of mind which is above and beyond the mental state which is needed concerning *Actus reus*[1]. In other words, the defendant must desire a specific result out of the illegal act and therefore, the prosecution must present specific proof to establish and satisfy this element. Specific intent crimes involve-

a. Attempt
b. Assault
c. Conspiracy
d. Burglary

3. Criminal Negligence/Recklessness- certain crimes require neither general intent nor any sort of specific intent. A prosecutor can seek conviction by establishing that the defendant acted recklessly or negligently. Recklessness s a more serious crime as compared to negligence.Thestandardsandchargesforbothvaryfromstatetostate.The conviction for recklessness can be illustrated in cases involving drag racing. The accused was convicted for illegal drag racing above the speed of forty miles per hour speed limit which as a result, led to negligent homicide. The court was of the view that "drag racing at such a speed exhibited such disregard for the interest of others as to amount to a gross deviation below the standard of care expected of a reasonably careful man."

[1]*People v. Hood*, 462 P.2d 370, 378 (Cal. 1969)

CHAPTER FIVE

Strict Liability

This is another segment of crimes that do not require the element of *Mens rea* to prove the guilt of a person. Strict liability crimes are also called 'Public Welfare Offences'. In such cases, the defendant is held liable simply because he committed such a crime. The laws relating to strict liability crimes are quite stringent and are meant to safeguard a certain class of people from undertaking certain kinds of conduct[1]. Strict liability crimes involve-

1. Statutory rape
2. Bigamy
3. Selling liquor to minors

The question of whether or not a crime comes under the purview of a strict liability crime is determined by the state legislature.

Presence of Mens rea under the Indian Penal Code, 1860

Although the word *Mens rea* is not mentioned under the Indian Penal Code, 1860, certain words still mark the existence of the term '*Mens rea*' in the above-mentioned statute. The words include the following–

1.Fraudulently– in a general sense, fraud refers to the intentional falsification concerning the material fact of a thing. Section 25 of the Indian Penal Code, 1860 states,"*A person is said to do a thing fraudulently if he does that thing with the intent to defraud but not otherwise.*" In other words, the offence of fraud cannot take place without an intention to defraud. Moreover, the offence of fraud can be pulled off in three ways-

- By deprivation of the rights of a person by either procuring something using deception or, by taking something without the owner's awareness or consent.

- By unlawfully holding on to something due for another person or stopping someone from detaining something that can be lawfully claimed by him.
- By unlawfully restraining or defeating another's right to property.

1.1 Essentials of fraud

- Deception or an intent to deceive; secrecy.
- Actual or possible injury or an intention to expose another person to actual injury or the risk of possible injury; using deception or secrecy.

In the case of Queen-Empress v. Soshi Bhushan,[2]the accused applied for admission to Benaras University in LL.B. final year. He stated that he had completed his previous study from the Lucknow Canning University and was, therefore, asked to produce a certification of having passed the examination for previous years. The accused produced a forged certificate and was liable for acting 'fraudulently'.

In the case of Dr. Vimla v. Delhi Administration,[3]the former was held liable for deceit. She portrayed herself to be Nalini and signed all the necessary documents required by the insurance company in that name. However, there was no advantage or non-economic loss or injury faced by the insurance company. In this case, the accused was not held liable for forgery under section467 and 468 of the IPC, 1860. This is because there was no injury or any sort of advantage to the accused. However, Dr. Vimla was held liable for committing the offence of fraud. The Supreme Court of India was of the view that the term 'defraud' is composed of two elements i.e. "deceit" and "injury" to the deceived person. Thus, even in the rarest of cases, if the deceiver is gaining some sort of benefit without any corresponding loss to the person deceived, the latter will be satisfied. The word "fraudulently" is mentioned under several sections of the Indian Penal Code, 1860, *viz..*, offences against "public justice (section 206-210)" or, offences concerned with "coins and Government stamps (section 246 & 247)" or, offences involving "weights and measures (section 264 & 265)etc.

2.Dishonestly– in simple words, dishonestly refers to 'untrustworthy, shameful, deceitful, or characterized by the lack of truth and honesty. 'Section 24 of the Indian Penal Code, 1860 describes 'dishonestly' as, "Whoever does anything intending to cause wrongful gain to one person or wrongful loss to another, is said to do that thing dishonestly."

Illustration– If 'A' is entitled to the possession of property from 'B' and the latter sues the former for outstanding rent, the basis of which is aren't noted, therefore, 'A' is said to act dishonestly as he is causing a wrongful gain to himself. In the case of Krishan Kumar v. Union of India,[4]the court held that an unlawful gain involves "wrongful retention" and unlawful loss involves "being kept out of the property in addition to, being wrongfully deprived of the property." Thus, whenever something passes onto the hands of the servant, he will be held liable for misappropriating any such thing under every circumstance which depicts the malicious intent to deprive the master of it.

*There are certain sections in the Indian Penal Code, 1860, wherein, the words 'fraudulently' and 'dishonestly' have collectively been used. The "sections are 209, 246, 247, 415, 421, 422, 423, 424, 464, 471 and 496."

3. Voluntarily- the word 'voluntarily' commonly means 'any act done with one's free will and without any sort of force or compulsion'. Section 39 of the Indian Penal Code, 1860 defines the word 'voluntarily' as, "A person is said to cause an effect voluntarily when he causes it by means which, at the time of employing those means, he knew or had reason to believe to be likely to cause it. "The section takes into consideration "knowledge" and "the reasonable grounds of belief", apart from intention. Therefore, offending voluntarily involves-

(a) "With the intention to cause the effect.

(b) With the knowledge of the likelihood of causing the effect.

(c) having reason to believe that the effect is likely to be caused."

In the case of Emperor v. Raghu Nath Rai,[5]a Hindu stole a calf from a Mohemmedon's house to protect it from slaughter. Here, the court held the accused guilty of theft and rioting irrespective of his pure motive of saving the calf from slaughter.

[1]*People v. Travers*, 124 Cal. Rptr. 728, 730 (1975)

[2]('93) ILR 15 All 210,1893 All WN 96

[3]AIR 1963 SC 1572: 1963 Supp (1) CR 585: (1963) 2 Cr LJ 434

[4]1959 AIR 1390, 1960 SCR (1) 452

[5](1892) 15 All 22

CHAPTER SIX

General Exceptions

As a general rule, a sane person is expected to know the nature of a particular act along with its consequences and therefore, is held responsible for the same. Nevertheless, there are certain exceptions to this rule, wherein a person may be exempted from any sort of criminal liability by holding a prestigious position and a high status such as the representative of a State or UN organization. However, others may be exempted from owing up to any sort of criminal liability due to the absence of the requisite *Mens rea* necessary for the commission of a particular crime. The makers of the Indian Penal Code, 1860 have thus, compiled all the cases relating to exceptions into one Chapter of the code i.e. Chapter IV (Sections 76-106) to prevent its repetition in every penal clause leading to several limitations. The chapter provides an extensive scope concerning the general exceptions. It not only takes into account the offences covered under the Penal Code but also includes the offences covered under the special and local laws in addition to, Section 40 of the Code. Chapter IV is inclusive of 31 sections which may be grouped under eight different heads, which are further compressed under the following two heads -

- Excusable Exceptions–here, the requisite *Mens rea* for a particular offence may be lacking either, because of a *bona fide* mistake concerning the existence of the fact (Section 76, 79), or if the act may be accidental (Section 80), or due to infancy (Section 82, 83), or insanity (Section 84), or intoxication (Sections 85-86) and therefore, the doer is not to be held responsible for his Act.
- Justifiable Exceptions – under such exceptions, the committed offences call for a legal justification either by the reason of the offence being committed by a judge under the supervision of law (Section 77), or through the orders of the court (Section 78), or to prevent further

damage to a person or property under necessary circumstances (Section 81), or if the act was consensual (Section 87-89, 92), or when the harm is near to causing death or grievous injury, or by force/ coercion(Section 94), or to exercise the right of private defence (Sections 96-106), or if the nature of the act trivial (Section 95). In the above mentioned scenarios, the law would not take note of it and hence, there will not be any sort of criminal liability imposed on the accused.

CHAPTER SEVEN

Conclusion

Criminal law is primarily associated with outcomes emerging from a certain kind of human conduct. The ancient Latin maxim '*Actus non-facit reum, nisi mens sit rea*' remains unquestioned till date as a proclamation of a common principle which states that no person can be convicted of a crime until and unless, both the requirements '*actus reus*' and '*mens rea*' are established in the committed crime. The burden of proof lies on the prosecutor and he must prove every element of a crime involving a criminal liability 'beyond reasonable doubt' to reflect the ordinary structure of criminal law. The abovementioned doctrines (*actus reus & mens rea),* distinguished from each other, are considered to be the two discrete elements of a crime. *Mens rea* is a broad concept and exists in several forms, depending upon the nature of the crime. And thus, the existence of several levels of *mens rea* such as"negligence, recklessness, knowledge, and purpose. "Based on these levels, the court takes into consideration the extent of criminal intent to convict a person for an offence. To undertake one's conviction, there exist different statutory provisions along with their object. The importance of *mens rea* in the Indian Penal Code, 1860 is associated with social and welfare statutes. The laws in force are enacted for the greater good of society. Questioning the existence of *mens rea* to punish the offenders for violating such enactments, may affect the ultimate goal of such Acts, or might as well defeat the object for its enactment.

9 798885 210508

Printed by Libri Plureos GmbH in Hamburg, Germany